T0199001

Why I Thank God

Porque le Doy Gracias a Dios

Written and Illustrated by

Grace Young

WestBow Press books may be ordered through booksellers or by contacting:

WestBow Press
A Division of Thomas Nelson & Zondervan
1663 Liberty Drive
Bloomington, IN 47403
www.westbowpress.com
844-714-3454

ISBN: 979-8-3850-0329-7 (sc)
ISBN: 979-8-3850-0330-3 (e)

Library of Congress Control Number: 2023913339

Print information available on the last page.

WestBow Press rev. date: 10/26/2023

WESTBOW
PRESS®
A DIVISION OF THOMAS NELSON
& ZONDERVAN

This story is about a little boy who owes all of his blessings to God. He comes from a religious family. He doesn't quite have a full understanding of God yet, but he does know that He exists. He is very thankful for the blessings he has received.

Esta historia es acerca de un niño que le debe todas sus bendiciones a Dios. El viene de una familia religiosa. El aún no tiene un entendimiento completo de lo que es Dios, pero sabe que Él existe. El está muy agradecido por las Bendiciones que ha recibido.

This book is dedicated to Tracey, Crystal, Michele, and Larmont Young Jr.

I thank God for the sun that shines.

Le doy gracias a Dios por el sol que brilla.

I thank God for the pretty blue sky.

Le doy gracias a Dios por el hemoso cielo azul.

I thank God for the
birds that sing.

*Le doy gracias a Dios por
los pajaros que cantan.*

I thank God for the pretty flowers.

Le doy gracias a Dios por las flores hermosas.

I thank God for my brother.

*Le doy gracias a Dios
por mi hermano.*

I thank God for my sister.

*Le doy gracias a Dios
por mi hermana.*

I thank God for my mother and father.

Le doy gracias a Dios por mi mamá y mi papá.

I thank God for my cat.

Le doy gracias a Dios por mi gato.

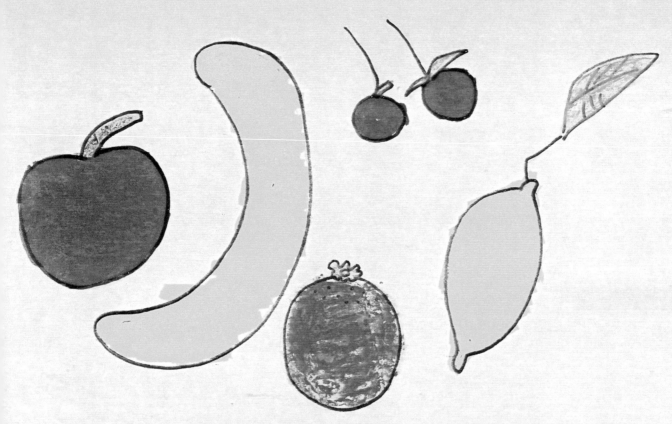

I Thank God for the food we eat.

Le doy gracias a Dios por la comida que comemos.

I thank God for the clothes we wear.

Le doy gracias a Dios por la ropa que usamos.

I thank God
for the trees.
*Le doy gracias
a Dios por
los árboles.*

**I thank God for
my church.**

*Le doy gracias a Dios
por mi Iglesia.*

I thank God for my school.

Le doy gracias a Dios por mi escuela.

I thank God
for my house.
*Le doy gracias
a Dios por
mi casa.*

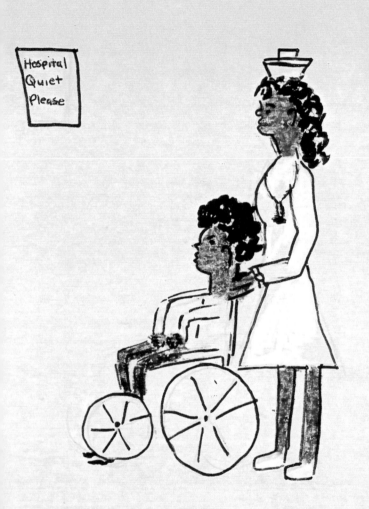

I thank God for the doctors and nurses.

Le doy gracias a Dios por los doctores y las enfermeras.

**And last but not lease,
I thank God for me.**

*Y por último le doy
gracias a Dios por mi.*

Grace Young Biography

I was born in Port Chester, New York and attended the Port Chester-Rye Union Free School District, and graduated from the Port Chester High School in 1968. I am a widow and was Married to Mr. Larmont Young, from Tuckahoe, New York who passed away in 1980. We have four children, Tracey, Crystal, Michele, and Larmont Young Jr.

I earned my Bachelor's Degree in Psychology with minor in Elementary Education and a Master of Science Degree in Education (Reading). I also hold permanent certificates in Education and Reading from the College of New Rochelle and a certificate of Theology from Oral Roberts University in Tulsa Oklahoma. I also earned a A.A.S. Degree in Nursing from Pace University in Pleasantville, New York. I also earned a Preacher's License from Charis Bible College, Beacon, New York Campus in May 2023.

I started working for the Port Chester-Rye Union Free School District as a Substitute Teacher and did so for 13 years. I was a teacher of Adult Basic Education in Math and Reading from 1974-1977, taught kindergarten at Thomas A. Edison Elementary School for a few years. I have been a substitute nurse for the District and also a tutor. I held the following position for the next 23 years as a Reading Specialist at Corpus Christi Holy Rosary School until I retired in 2013.

I am very active in the Port Chester Community. I am a member of the American Red Cross Disaster Services and have been a member for 25 years and still involved with them. The Port Chester Teacher Association, and W.E.V.R.C. (Westchester Emergency Volunteer Reserve Corp) as a volunteer nurse. I was a volunteer at United Hospital in the Emergency Room until the hospital closed in 2005. I was also a volunteer at Greenwich Hospital in the Emergency Room.

I am a member of St. Frances A.M.E. Zion Church, where I held the following positions: Chairman of the Trustee Board from the year 2012 for six years, Assistant Superintendent of the Sunday School, a Sunday School Teacher, W.H.O.M. (Women's Home and Overseas Missionary Society), Church Health Medical Staff Member. I have been volunteering in the church soup kitchen for over 25 years and also participated as a volunteer at Corpus Christi Church for the Midnight Run (a program that goes out and feeds the homeless who are living in the streets (bringing food and clothing) I am also a member of the N.A.A.C.P.

I am also a volunteer at Don Bosco Community Center with their outreach program passing out food and clothing to the needy.

I received Proclamations October 15, 2016 from the following : Westchester County Board of Legislators, Port Chester, New York, Town of Rye Westchester County New York, Port Chester-Rye N.A.A.C.P. Freedom Fund Luncheon Award Meritorious Activities Received awards from George Latimer, New York State Senate, New York State Assembly Citation (State Assemblyman) Steven Otis, Office of County Executive Westchester County, New York Robert Asterino, (County Executive) Award, Honorary Teacher Retirement of Outstanding Accomplishments June 19, 2013 Superintendent of Schools Dr. Edward Kliszus

Award certificate with the American Red Cross for 25 years of service volunteering March 25, 2021

I received a Citation March 25, 2021 from Assemblyman, Steven Otis

I am the proud grandmother of seven grandchildren and four great grandchildren. In my leisure time I love reading, dabbling in clay arts, bicycle riding, ice skating and walking on nice days.

I strongly believe that the children are our future. I believe in what the Bible says (Proverbs 22:6) "Train up a child in the way he should go: and when he is old, he will not depart from it"

Printed in the United States
by Baker & Taylor Publisher Services